HAPPY NEW YEAR

HAPPY NEW YEAR

by **Emily Kelley**
pictures by **Priscilla Kiedrowski**

CAROLRHODA
ON MY OWN BOOKS

Carolrhoda Books
Minneapolis, Minnesota

For Charlie

Manufactured in the United States of America

This book is available in two editions:
Library binding by Carolrhoda Books, Inc.
Soft cover by First Avenue Editions
241 First Avenue North
Minneapolis, Minnesota 55401

Library of Congress Cataloging in Publication Data

Kelley, Emily.
Happy New Year   **074864**
    (A Carolrhoda on my own book)
    Summary: Describes the way in which the new year is
celebrated throughout the world, often on days other
than January 1.
    1. New Year—Juvenile literature. [1. New Year]
I. Kiedrowski, Priscilla, ill. II. Title. III. Series.

GT4905.K44   1984 394.2'683 84-5020
ISBN 0-87614-269-2 (lib. bdg.)
ISBN 0-87614-469-5 (pbk.) $14.95

      5   6   7   8   9   10   97   96   95   94   93   92   91   90

Contents

Ecuador: *Año Viejo*   7

Iran: *No Ruz*   11

Japan   19

Jewish: *Rosh Hashanah*   22

Vietnam: *Tet Nguyen Dan*   27

Sierra Leone   32

China   36

Map   40

Some Other Customs   42

New Year's Jokes and Games   44

The Wassail Bowl   45

Wassailing the Fruit Trees   46

Glossary   48

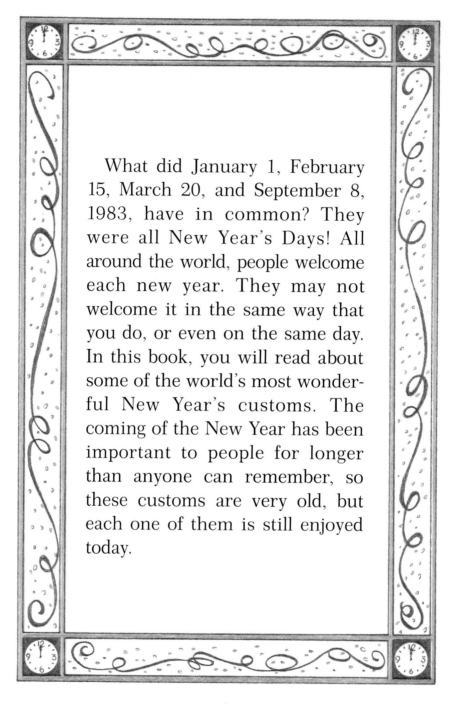

What did January 1, February 15, March 20, and September 8, 1983, have in common? They were all New Year's Days! All around the world, people welcome each new year. They may not welcome it in the same way that you do, or even on the same day. In this book, you will read about some of the world's most wonderful New Year's customs. The coming of the New Year has been important to people for longer than anyone can remember, so these customs are very old, but each one of them is still enjoyed today.

In Ecuador, South America,
December 31 is called *Año Viejo*
(AHN-yo vee-AY-ho).
That means "Old Year."
On Old Year,
most families have an extra member—
a scarecrow!

Someone gives him a shirt.
Someone else may give him a hat.
Others may give him pants
or a pipe or a cane.
The family stuffs the clothes
with straw.
Then they place the old man
on a chair outdoors.
The children dance around him.
Someone writes a will for him.
The will is a list
of everyone's faults.
At midnight, the will is read.
Everyone laughs.

9

Finally, a match is lit.
Poof! The old man and his will
go up in flames.
And so, they say,
do the family's faults.
Everyone will start
the new year fresh.
Last year's faults
will all be forgotten.

In Iran, New Year is called *No Ruz*
(no ROOZ).

No Ruz begins on March 20.

It lasts for 13 days.

It comes in March
because spring begins in March.

Several weeks before March 20,

people plant tiny gardens in bowls.

11

12

They clean their houses.
Children get new clothes.
The evening before *No Ruz* begins,
the family eats together.
They eat the same meal every year:
eggs and a rice dish called pilaf
(PEE-lahf).
This meal is supposed to
bring good luck.
After the meal, friends often visit.
They bring gifts of fruit,
flowers, and colored eggs.

Late that night,
the family sits around a table.
Everyone has a colored egg
and a mirror.
Iranians say that the earth shakes
when the new year begins.
At that exact moment,
everyone puts an egg on a mirror.
The eggs begin to shake!
Is the earth really shaking?
Or are the eggs shaking
because of all the cannons
going off?

At last it's time to feast
on chicken, fruits,
bread, and sweets.
Finally, someone reads
from the Koran.
The Koran is a holy book.
Then it's time for bed.

The 13th day of *No Ruz*
is called *Sizdah Bi Dar*
(seez-dah bay DAHR).
This means "13th Day Out."
Iranians say it is unlucky
to stay indoors then.
They pack picnic lunches.
Then they set off into the country.
Children bring their bowl gardens.

They throw them into country streams.
They say that they are
throwing away bad luck.
So ends *No Ruz* for another year.

In Japan, New Year's Day
comes on January 1.
People decorate their houses
for the New Year.
They hang pine branches or bamboo
beside their front doors.
These stand for health and long life.

They hang ropes over their doors.
They tie them around
their water wells.
They lay them over their roofs.
They hang seaweed, ferns, and fans
from the ropes.
These things stand for happiness
and good luck.
On New Year's Eve,
most grown-ups stay up
to hear the gong.
It rings 108 times.
The moment the New Year comes,
Japanese people begin to laugh.
They laugh and laugh.
This is supposed to bring them
good luck in the new year.

Jewish people have two New Years.
One is their country's New Year.
The other is the Jewish New Year.
It is called *Rosh Hashanah*
(roash huh-SHOW-nuh).
Rosh Hashanah usually comes
in September.
It lasts for one or two days.
It begins at sundown on one day.
It ends at sundown
one or two days later.
On *Rosh Hashanah*,
everyone goes to the synagogue.
A ram's horn is blown.
It reminds people
to think about last year's sins.

At home, a special prayer
is said before the evening meal.
It is called the *Kiddush*
(kih-DOOSH).
Candles are lit.
Other prayers are said.
Someone dips a piece of apple
into honey.
That person says,
"May it be God's will
to grant us a good and sweet year."

Rosh Hashanah begins
10 days of prayer and worship.
Those 10 days end
with *Yom Kippur*
(YOAM kih-PUHR).
On *Yom Kippur*,
Jewish people do not eat.
They worship God.
They pray to become better people.
When *Yom Kippur* is over,
they are ready to start a new year.

In Vietnam the New Year is called
Tet Nguyen Dan (tet nwin dahng),
or *Tet* for short.
Tet begins between
January 21 and February 19.
The exact day changes
from year to year.

The Vietnamese people believe
that gods live in their houses.
The gods protect the family.
On *Tet*, families say good-bye
to their kitchen gods.
They believe the gods
are going to heaven.
There they will report on the family.
Of course, everyone wants
a good report.
So before *Tet* begins,
families give presents to their gods.
When *Tet* arrives,
they set off firecrackers.
The gods leave for heaven
with a bang.

Tet lasts for three days.

During this time, people light candles
for their dead relatives.

They believe their dead relatives
come back during *Tet*.

People give presents to the gods
who protect their tools.

Farmers may leave out food

for the gods who protect their plows.
Carpenters may give flowers
to the gods who protect
their hammers and saws.
During *Tet*
everyone tries to be happy.
If they are not,
it could bring bad luck.

In Sierra Leone, Africa,

crops are not grown

during the dry season.

In March or April, the rains begin.

New life comes to the land.

That is why some Mandingo people

(man-DING-go)

welcome the New Year at this time.

The dry season ends.

It is planting time again.

On New Year's Eve,
people clean their houses.
They sweep their yards.
They gather all their buckets together.

On New Year's Day,
women and children
meet in the village.
They sing and dance
to the music of drums and flutes.

The men go to a stream.
They fill all the buckets.
They place the buckets on their heads.
Then they march back to the village.
The people are showing their thanks
for the rain that will soon come.

The Chinese believe
that the Old Year gets tired.
It goes away
so that the New Year can come.
This happens sometime
in January or February.
The most wonderful part
of Chinese New Year
is the Festival of Lanterns.
On that day,
all of the offices are closed.
Children wear new clothes.
People eat special foods.
Lanterns are everywhere.
They light the way for the New Year.

That night,
fireworks go off.
There is a huge parade
with thousands of lanterns
and a giant paper dragon.

38

The Chinese welcome the New Year
with great happiness.
It is time to look ahead
to a brand new year.

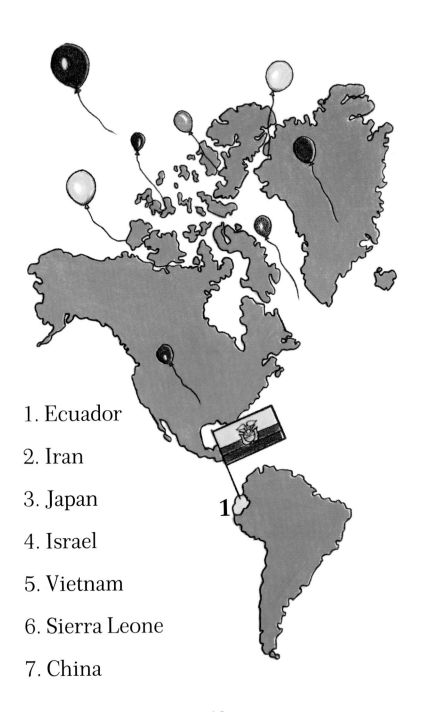

1. Ecuador

2. Iran

3. Japan

4. Israel

5. Vietnam

6. Sierra Leone

7. China

41

Some Other Customs

Belgium
Early on New Year's Day, Belgian farmers go out to their barns and wish their animals a Happy New Year.

France
In France, people eat pancakes on New Year's Day to bring them good luck for the rest of the year.

Switzerland
For their good luck, people in Switzerland let a drop of cream fall to the floor on New Year's Day.

42

Puerto Rico

Watch out if you're in Puerto Rico on New Year's Eve! You might get wet! Children throw pails of water out their windows at midnight. This is supposed to get rid of any evil spirits in their houses.

Spain

When the clock strikes 12 on New Year's Eve, Spanish people eat 12 grapes! Each stroke of the clock stands for one month in the year. Each grape brings good luck for that month.

Greece

Children in Greece are especially lucky. On New Year's Eve, St. Basil fills their shoes with presents. At midnight, the children open their presents and welcome the new year.

Laugh it up!

Many people around the world think that laughing on New Year's Eve will bring good luck. Here are some riddles to tell your friends. If they laugh, maybe you will have brought them good luck.

1. Why is the calendar sad on New Year's Eve?
2. What did the shy clock do on New Year's Eve?
3. Why did the teacher throw his clock out the window?
4. What did the minute hand say to the second hand?

Answers: 1. Because its days are numbered. 2. It kept its hands in front of its face. 3. He wanted to see time fly. 4. I'll be around in an hour.

Pick a resolution!

Here's a game to play with your friends on New Year's Day. Have each person write a silly New Year's resolution on a piece of paper. Fold the papers in half. Put them all into a hat. Now pass the hat around. Everyone must draw a resolution from the hat and follow it for the rest of the day.

The Wassail Bowl

In Merry Old England, families drank from the "wassail bowl" on New Year's Day. The bowl was filled with a hot, spicy drink. Somewhere in the bowl was a ring. Each person was given a cup of the drink. Then the head of the house said, "Waes-hail!" That means, "Be in good health!" The others answered, "Drink-hail!" and drank from their cups. If the ring was in your cup, it meant you would get married in the new year.

Here is a recipe for your wassail bowl.

2 cups apple juice

⅓ cup lemon juice

2 cups cranberry juice

¼ cup sugar

2 cups tea

2 sticks cinnamon

1 cup orange juice

6 whole cloves

Mix everything in a large pot. Simmer for ½ hour. Remove the cinnamon sticks and cloves. You can serve your wassail from a punch bowl or right from the pot. Make sure it's warm. (Serves 10)

Wassailing the Fruit Trees

Another English custom was "wassailing the fruit trees." All the young boys got up early on New Year's Day. They hurried out to the orchards. From tree to tree they marched. They stood around each one and beat it with branches. All the while, they sang a song much like the one on the next page.

These boys were called "howlers." People believed they made the trees bear more fruit in the new year.

Here's to Thee, Old Apple Tree!

Traditional English

Here's to thee, old ap - ple tree,

Here's to thee, old ap - ple tree!

Give us a crop Of good ap - ples ripe,

Red and well- roun - ded The good jui - cy type!

Hats full! Caps full! Good bush - el - sacks full! My

pock - ets too, Hur - rah! Was - sail!

47

Glossary

bamboo (bam-BOO): a kind of plant with a long, hard stem

cannon (KAN-un): a very big gun

carpenter (KAR-pen-tur): a person who builds things out of wood

fern (FURN): a kind of green plant

festival (FESS-tih-vul): a big party

gong (GONG): a flat bell, shaped like a saucer, that is rung by hitting it with a padded hammer

Koran (KORE-an): the bible for Muslim people

lantern (LAN-turn): a kind of light that can be carried easily

pilaf: (PEE-lahf): a dish made of rice with meat and spices

seaweed (SEE-weed): a plant that grows in the sea

synagogue (SINN-ah-gog): a church for Jewish people

will (WILL): a piece of paper that says what should be done with a person's money and belongings after the person dies

worship (WERE-shup): the way people follow their religions